KENNETH LEE
McKELLAR M.A.

I WANT TO
BE GOOD

"A *CREATIVE* LOOK AT APPROACHING LIFE"

Chance In Time Press

Printed in the United States of America.
ISBN 0-9657317-0-7
Published by: Chance In Time Press
                  P.O. Box 1548
                  Frederick, Maryland 21702

This book is dedicated to Jen McKellar, my wife and friend who has been a tremendous source of strength throughout our ten years of marriage and then some. Jen ,thanks for the guidance and support on this project as well as the others. As this manuscript is handed down to our children, this book is dedicated to you, through me, for them.

Acknowledgements

I would first like to thank my Mom and Dad, who always believed in me, and continue to be a guide in my life. The love and support that they have given me throughout my life has helped mold me in the direction of good. Mom, Dad thank you and I love you. I am indebted to my brothers, Don, Larry, Keith and my youngest brother and hero Patrick. I could not have picked a better family, even if I had a magic wand. Thanks to John and Odetta Lake my inlaws who believed in me and laughed at my jokes. I am grateful to Robert Boyle, Wanda Ruffin, Theresa Akney, and Margaret Burke who read my manuscript and gave me friendly criticism. A special thanks and a shoutout to Terri Tucker who has helped in more ways than one with this book. You are truly a friend. Leslie, thank you, thank you, thank you. Thanks for believing in me, Carol, Emily, and all of the people at Pathways. Thanks Michael Clark for managing and bringing this project to fruition. There have been so many people in my life that have helped me along the way I can't begin to mention them all. Thank you, to everyone.

Mr. Trotman, you made a difference.

KENNETH LEE McKELLAR M.A.

I WANT TO BE GOOD

Emily,
Thank you for bring out the best in
me. thank for the support and the
directions. Emily you are great—

Ky L McKellar

"A *CREATIVE* LOOK AT APPROACHING LIFE"

Introduction

•

Each day that we walk on this planet, we have decisions that we make. We decide what clothes to wear or the group of friends we are going to hang around. From the time we are very young we are being molded into a particular type of person. That person is constantly changing because our experiences change. Every day we have a chance to start over, to change. As we grow into our teens, we start to form ourselves and reach for what we want to be. We start to make decisions about the type of person we want to become . The actions you take today will determine the person you will become tomorrow. Think about what you want out of life. Who do you want to be? What kind of mark will you make on this earth? It all starts with your future's past. What we do today determines the stand we make tomorrow. What we think about influences our future actions. Hi, I am Kenneth Lee McKellar and **I Want To Be Good**.

The reason I chose to write this book and use this title relates to my childhood. I grew up in New Jersey with four brothers, my mother, and my father. My parents were very hard working, stern disciplinarians. They provided me with guidance and direction. In spite of all the action in the McKellar household we always found time to have fun. Some of the most influential events in my life took place

•

when I was thirteen. My father worked the evening shift at Ford Motor Company in Edison, New Jersey. He did not get home from work until around 1:00 in the morning. Often I had difficulty sleeping through the night, as I still do today. The warm milk thing just didn't seem to help. I would wake up in the wee hours of the morning and go downstairs to grab a bite to eat. I was usually searching for the chocolate chip cookies. Dad was getting home about this time. My mother always had a plate of food in the oven waiting for him. As Dad waited for dinner to warm up in the oven, it gave us time to talk. When he got home, Dad would ask me to turn on the television. My youngest brother Patrick was sleeping, so I was the TV remote. I had to raise off the favorite chair and turn the television to one of the three channels that were still on at that hour. The two of us would catch the last part of the late, late movie. Most of the time the movie was a western. I remember enjoying the Clint Eastwood westerns most. This was long before the days of *Pale Rider* and *In the Line of Fire.* In the old westerns, Clint would get beaten almost to death and still come back to beat up the bad guys.

What I remember most about these times is the joy of being alone with my father. My four brothers were asleep and my mom was resting. I recall watching the movies, *Fist Full of Dollars*, and *The Good, the Bad and the Ugly* and saying, "Dad, the bad guys are going to get the gold". With the voice of confidence Dad would say, "You can't keep a good man down". I would reply, "Dad, what are you talking about? They just shot him. His rebuttal was always the same, "You can't keep a good man down." I was persistent with Dad saying; "You can't shoot a man in the chest, beat down his gun slinging hand, and expect him to have the gumption to redeem himself. This movie is over!" My father's verbal retaliation was the same, "You can't keep a good man down," Sure enough, Clint would put a metal shield over his chest, practice shooting with his left hand, and come back and be victorious in his quest to regain the gold or whatever he had lost. You can't keep a good man down. This guiding principle has governed my thoughts throughout my life. Now I write about the journey of being good. The root of this principle is that we can be all that we aspire to be in life. As I look to where I am going, I write from where I have been. A child of special educational programs, some of my teachers felt that I would not even graduate high school. The people that I looked up to looked down on my future. When I was in high school my first guidance counselor told me the only thing that I could hope to do in college was fail. She was wrong, I am not a writer by training, yet I write. We can be all that we desire to be.

When you read this book, I have some requests. One is that you take your time and really enjoy this book. Have fun as you learn and make changes in your life. This book reflects my personality, who I am. A man in the process of being good. As you read, take your time and allow yourself to develop an image of who you seek to become. Often, I find myself building a relationship with the author as I read and try to ponder the author's thoughts. As you read this book, you may feel refreshed and rejuvenated. Please, go on and enjoy yourself. This book is about looking at self. It is about fulfilling life, reaching goals, and enjoying success. Ask 100 wise men what success is and you will get 100 wise answers. Your answer will be just as wise. Walk with me and journey into ***I WANT TO BE GOOD: A CREATIVE LOOK AT APPROACHING LIFE***.

"*The change in your environment starts with your internal self*"

---•---

I WANT TO
BE GOOD

Contents

CHAPTER 1
Why Good *1*

CHAPTER 2
Mind Power *9*

CHAPTER 3
C*hildhood* *13*

CHAPTER 4
R*elations* *19*

CHAPTER 5
E*xcitement* *31*

CHAPTER 6
A*spirations* *37*

CHAPTER 7
T*ransformation* *43*

CHAPTER 8
I*ncessant* *47*

CHAPTER 9
V*ehicle* *55*

CHAPTER 10
E*mpowerment* *59*

CHAPTER 11
Just Good *64*

Why Good?

C H A P T E R   I

As a child I grew up in Princeton, New Jersey, and went through the Princeton school system. In high school I participated in several sports. I was active all year round. An incident that had a powerful impact on my life took place in the 9th grade. During the spring of my freshman year I was participating in track and field as a high jumper. I was fortunate enough to participate at the varsity level as a freshman. The night before a dual meet with a local high school team, I couldn't sleep. I was nervous and had all kinds of thoughts rolling around my brain. I was going to compete in the high jump. As I often did, I came downstairs in the middle of the night to get a snack. I sat down in the family's favorite chair. As I mentioned in the introduction, I have four brothers, a mother and a father. Everybody in the family loved to sit in this raggedy old green chair. It was extremely comfortable. No matter whose butt was in this chair it would magically conform, making the chair and butt as one. It was the most comfortable chair I ever had the pleasure of plopping on. If you ever fell asleep in this chair, you had good dreams. The kind of dreams that brings drool to your lips and down your chin. This was a good chair! I was sitting in the chair, leaning back waiting for Dad. I was thinking of the track meet and how I wanted to be the best. My Dad was due

"It's not where you think you are... it's where you think you are going."

————•————

I WANT TO
BE GOOD

in from work at any time. On many nights we would sit up talking about life. Dad came in from work, got his food out of the oven and immersed himself in eating. I didn't say anything. At first Dad was also silent. Finally, he asked what was wrong. I said, "Nothing, I just can't sleep." He then asked me if I was ready for the meet. I said, "Yes, but I'm not expecting to win. After all I'm just a freshman, with the best highjumper in the state on my team." As Dad was sipping his milk he said, "You go out there and do a good job," and I said "But I want to be great." My father said, "All you need to be is good." I asked "Why good?"

What my father shared with me, I will always remember. He said, "Great is a moment, good is forever; great is an event, good is a lifetime. Great is an aspect of your life, a portion of you in your life; a sport, a song, a composition. Good is you throughout your life. If you are good from day to day in the end you will be one of the few, which is great." His words simply did not penetrate my brain. It just did not connect for me. It was as though the neurons were shooting into space. I thought my Dad had lost all the red cards out of his deck, maybe he was working too hard. How can "good" be "great" in the end? I didn't understand his words, but I did remember them. Later, as I was going through life, I began looking at "good" and how people evaluated "good." I looked at how people defined "good" versus other words such as fantastic, awesome, great, super, and terrific. Somebody can make a great catch in the Super Bowl game, hit three home runs in a play off game, like Reggie Jackson and people will say he was awesome. Franco Harris once made a catch in a football play-off game that came to be called the immaculate reception. This one moment is merely a fraction of the many moments that compose a lifetime. When I talk about "good" I am speaking of the day to day efforts that make up that one immaculate moment. Life is not made up of one event. It takes a life time of events to write the chapters of our lives. Great is made up of many good efforts.

WHY "GOOD"? The word good has been around for many years. According to the Bible, during the start of mankind, the word good was used. Look in the book of Genesis. God talked about earth and creating earth, and saw it was good. God created wind, sunlight and dark. After creating these things, he saw they were good and said they were good. God then created man. After creating man God said it was good, saw it was good, and so it was good. When you look in the Bible you see the word "good" referred to in the same context as man. A "good" man.

The reason I have devoted a whole chapter to "good" is because I think many times as we are going through life, we have a tendency to be philosophical about accomplishing our goals. We tend to look at ourselves or other people and put them on a pedestal that is not stable; or a very weak pedestal that can be easily knocked down. If we put ourselves or an event or goal on a level far greater than ourselves it is hard to visualize success. However, when we put our efforts into being as good as we are capable, day in and day out, we can reach the best in ourselves. We can shoot for the goals that are within us. There are often awesome events nature brings into our lives. Examples include: the healing of a wound or giving birth to a child. Good is defined in a way which can only be assessed at the end of an event. So, if we are talking about humans, we can only define good at the end of our stay on earth. Being a good person is a continuous pursuit. It doesn't happen in a day or a year, it occurs over a lifetime.

Whether you are on this earth ten, twenty or fifty years the final evaluation will be made when you are in the box, ashes or however your body is disposed of when you are gone. If you do right by yourself, do right by your family, nature, and all those who you come in contact with, your evaluation will be a favorable one. In the end you will be great. As we go through life we have two choices. We can take this life one day at a time. We can define who we want to be as a person and go after our dreams. This is the mission of the "good."

The other thing we can do is sit back and wait for a gift in life.

Before you can fly with Superman you have to walk with the good in you. Come to think of it, good is all Superman wanted to be. I realize Superman is a fictitious character but, let's talk about the man called Super. Here was a man running around in pajamas with a big S on his chest. The man wore a bath robe on his back, going around helping people. Don't forget he could fly. Superman wasn't from this world. He was from Krypton. When he was a baby (stay with me on this, I do have a point) his planet was going to blow up. His father knew the planet was going to explode, so he tried to build a rocket ship for his family. Doomsday came before the rocket was ready for the family so his father sent his only son to Earth. His father hoped his son would be safe because the blast from the explosion would give the baby superhuman powers. After the baby landed on earth he was found by a family and appeared to be just like any other baby. He could have been found by anybody. Whoever found him would have a great impact on his life. The family that found him was the Kent's. They adopted him and named him Clark. The Kent's were law abiding citizens and raised Clark with the same values. When he was growing up Clark had tough times. He had girl troubles, school troubles, peer pressures, and poor grades. He had conflicts with his parents. His Dad did not think it was ethically correct for superman to play sports, Clark really wanted to play sports. Could you imagine superman playing basketball? He could jump right up and over Michael Jordan! He really wanted to play but he had his parents' values instilled in him. He knew it was his job to be good, to be helpful, and to use his powers to help mankind. Let me tell you how superman got his name. He didn't name himself. He didn't just get up one morning and say, "I am superman and I am going to save this planet by doing all the right things." The name superman was given to him by mortals. People looked at his unnatural strength and said "doggone this man is super," this man can do a lot of unnatural things. He can pick up cars, throw rocks really far, he can also fly. Superman was given the name super by other human beings. In reality superman just wanted to be good. He just wanted to do the right thing. He just wanted to be a good man and to get an "A" in spanish. Yes, I am a fan of superman because I think we all have inside of us not only the goodness, but the power to do anything we want. This is evident if you look at athletes.

Lets take a look at the long jumper Robert Beamon. Beamon was a 22 year old, six foot three, long jumper on the USA Olympics team. He participated in the 1968 Olympics in Mexico City. On a rainy day in Mexico City Bob Beamon ran down the long jump run way and appeared to take flight. Beamon did the impossible. The long jump world record was 27 feet 3/4 inches and it was held by Ralph Boston and Igor Ter-Ovanesyan. Bob Beamon smashed this world record. When the goal of the long jumper was to reach the 28 foot mark Beamon, on his first jump in the Olympic finals surpassed the world record. When he landed, the flight read 29 feet 2 1/2 inches. This was 21 and 3/4 inches better than the record. On this day in Mexico City Bob Beainon took flight. He jumped further than anyone had ever dreamed. Why GOOD? Because we possess, good in ourselves and if we tap into the goodness of ourselves we can unleash the powers many perceive as only belonging to superman.

WHY GOOD? Because good is great in the end. "Good" is a lifetime. "Good" is coming home from school with a poor report card, maybe even "F's", but going back the next day and trying to make better grades. "Good" is going back to the huddle after you just let the most important pass of the game slip through your hands. "Good" is going out for cheerleading and not making it, but trying again next year or trying another sport. "Good" is practicing a debate and working really hard but not making the final cut, and still coming back to be part of the team in some other role. "Good" are the leaders around us that have come from many diverse circumstances to get where they are, not because they gave up, but because they continued on about their dream and their destiny. "Good" is a state of mind, a power so awesome that it can reward us with a lifetime of enjoyment, happiness and satisfaction. Why "Good?" because good is within you and me. "Good" is all that we have to offer. "Good" is the positive efforts we put forth in our lives day-in and day-out. "Good" is within you and within you is greatness at the end.

"You are the vehicle to your destiny."

---•---

I WANT TO
BE GOOD

Mind Power

●

CHAPTER 2

The mind is a powerful tool composing thoughts that guide us. We are where we are based on our thinking. The thoughts that we hold onto determine our life's present situation. The brain is about three pounds of soft spongy tissue made up of millions of neurons. It has four parts called lobes. The parietal lobe deals with touch, pain, and temperature. The occipital lobe deals with vision. The temporal lobe deals with sound and smell. The frontal lobe receives sensory impulses from the other three lobes and then begins the process that signals and gives commands to the muscles. In other words if you touch a hot stove your parietal lobe will let your frontal lobe know that you touched something hot that causes pain. Your frontal lobe will send the message of pain to your finger tips and you will pull your hand away from the hot stove and the message will travel to your mouth and move your lips to say "Ouch, that hurts." This experience will be put into a small filing cabinet that says when I touch a hot stove pain comes and it makes me say, "Ouch, that hurts." These lobes are divided into hemispheres. There is a right hemisphere and a left hemisphere. The left hemisphere is responsible for the right hand touch, speech, language, writing, logic, math, and science. The right hemisphere is responsible for the spatial construction,

●

●

fantasies, art appreciation, and music appreciation. You have a super amount of action going on in the brain. Just think of your brain as an IBM office with departments all assigned separate territories with their own cubicles. The brain stores this activity in the memory so it can recall what has gone on. This leaves the body to carry out the commands of the brain.

The job of your body is to carry and protect the mind (brain). You are your mind, you are your thoughts. Your thoughts tell the rest of your body to walk and talk and even breathe. Your brain is the engine to the rest of your body, whether your body is green, yellow, black, red, big, small, short, or stout it is operated by the brain. As you walk on this planet, please note, you are not your body. You are your brain, your thoughts, your experiences. You are what you tell yourself you are. The brain is the engine and your body carries out the commands of your brain. Knowing that we are our brains, I have come to the conclusion that we act out our inner thoughts. The mind puts into perspective the past to arrive at the present in preparation for the future. In other words, our past experiences helped us get to where we are today. Today determines where we are going tomorrow. However we are not limited to our past experiences as a spring-board into the future. We can only limit ourselves by putting restrictions on our thinking.

Henry Ford said "Whether you think you can or think you can't, you are right." We will always have the stronger springs of today's present situation and experience to help us soar. This way we may surpass experiences and frustrations and realize our fantasies.

Throughout this book we are going to take a creative look at approaching life. The creative power that we can take out of our **childhood**. The creative powers we have in our **relationships**. The creative power we have inside ourselves to become **excited**. Being creative, to have dreams and **aspirations** to transform life into exactly what we want. This **transformation** does not come without

●

an **incessant** attitude. We are what powers us. We are the **vehicle** to our destiny. We have the ability to **empower** ourselves to greatness. It starts with the way we think about ourselves and the environment around us. The mind feeds on present experiences and proceeds through life with the aid of familiarities of the past. So as you take a creative look at approaching life, keep in mind that we are the products of our thoughts.

Knowing that we make up our thoughts, we need to be careful what we think about. If we spend our time thinking about all the negatives in other people, the ill will that we project onto others will become our own welcome mat. If you put down your world, you soon become the landing pad of your put downs. I once told my son Jonathan that he was acting like a clown. Jon said, "I am rubber and you are glue whatever you say bounces off of me and sticks to you." This is a saying that has been a favorite of mine for many years. Now my son has stuck it on me. The world can learn from Jon. Give out only what you want in return and you will get what you want.

"Where your mind goes, your body will follow"

---●---

I WANT TO
BE GOOD

Childhood

CHAPTER 3

I want to talk a bit about childhood in this book. Childhood is an experience you really have to take a look at and put into perspective. As a child it is your first time and only time going through the experience of childhood. It might also be the first time the person raising you is going through parenthood.

We experience a great deal as kids, but remember, we were young and had a childlike perspective and the people around us were learning too. Childhood is the first step in a creative look at approaching life. Childhood plays a tremendous part in who we are today. Whether you are reading this book in middle school, high school, or at age sixty-five, your childhood has had an impact on your life. There is, sometimes, a misconception about childhood and the effect it can have on life. Even though our childhood and past play an enormous role in where we are today they do not have to limit us where we are or in what we are doing. In other words, if at the age twenty-seven, you are down in the dumps because of your child-hood misfortunes, it doesn't necessarily mean you have to work in the junkyard of life.

Yes, many of your childhood woes will manifest themselves later in your life. However, your later life does not have to provide your childhood woes with the full exposure that you experienced as a child.

The wonderful thing about past events is that you can choose what you want to hold on to. When we think about the past or about an event that occurred during our childhood, many times we are not looking at that event from beginning to end. We do not even fully consider the particulars of the experience. We tend to draw from bits and pieces making a full conclusion today, based on pieces of experiences from yesterday. This can be beneficial if we use childhood events that helped us feel better about ourselves rather than the experiences that lead into a perpetual state of pain. If you had a terrible childhood, you have the ability to draw from some little piece of good that happened and use it for a parachute in your adult life. This can help weed out all the negative thoughts that lower your self-esteem. The goal is to be the best that you can be. Being the best that you can be is being good. When I speak of being the best you can be, I'm talking about all that you can be at any given time.

Being good requires emotional work. This emotional work starts when we realize that we are not going in the direction we want to go. It starts when we feel that the habits that we have built for ourselves no longer work and that our thinking is not productive. Childhood is a part of life that everybody experiences. There are tools that we learn to use as children that protect us as children, but are not effective for us as adults. For instance, as a young boy one of the most important lessons I was taught was not to talk to strangers or get in a car with strangers. This was handed down to me from my parents as a form of protection.

As a child, this was good advice. But as an adult, being shy or wary of people is not going to help me as a professional speaker. In fact, to be successful I have to talk to people that I don't know. Buried deep inside of me is the notion that I should keep to myself for protection. This mechanism didn't help me, so I had to break through that wall of protection.

This is what you have to do. You have to break through all the barriers keeping you from going where you want to go and being who you want to be. You have to break through what I call the elephant phenomenon. The reason I call it the elephant phenomenon is because I took my three sons to the circus and there were three elephants in one ring. We noticed that the elephants were being handled by string. Jon said to Kevin, "Look they are holding the elephants with just string." Kevin said, "No way Jon, the elephants could just break the string and come up here and eat all of us." Kevin started to get scared so they said "Dad, How is that little string holding those big elephants?" I didn't know the answer so I said, "Be quiet and watch the show." I figured I could find the answer to that question another time. Later, I heard Michael Clark explain the elephant phenomenon. During the training of baby elephants they have a huge chain around their legs. They can't break through this huge chain, but they try and they fail, they try again and they fail, and whenever they try they fail. No matter what they do, they can not break through that chain. As they grow older, they stop trying and the trainer puts smaller and smaller chains on them. By the time they are adults, the trainer puts only a small rope on them. The elephants don't even try to break the rope because they have learned as young elephants that they can not break free. What they learned as baby elephants is not true for the adult elephants, but they don't know that. As adults they have the strength to break through that rope, but they don't realize that they could walk right out of the tent to the concession stand and demand peanuts. They are **limited** by their childhood thinking. This thinking keeps them tied to that rope that could barely hold a decent size dog.

This is also true for the way adults talk to children or the way you were talked to as a child. If, as a child, you were always told that you were smart, smart, smart you will grow up thinking that you are smart.

If as a child you were always told that you were good looking, you are going to walk with charm in your step. If you were told that you are stubborn, stubborn, stubborn, then you will go around being stubborn. I have a child named Stephen who is one of the most stubborn people on the face of this earth. I don't know if he is just stubborn, or if the age of two is synonymous with being stubborn. However, it is all right to be stubborn, some of the best business men in the world are stubborn. Most successful lawyers are stubborn. Stubborn can be a good quality. I want Stephen to be stubborn as he says no to drugs. Stubborn is great as he walks away from violence. However, it is the reaction of the adults in our life that help determine how this quality of stubbornness will be used later in life. Will it be good or bad? I call these qualities gifts. If we use these gifts correctly they can help reap many rewards. These gifts used incorrectly often bring consequences that come in through the back door often producing awkward circumstances. Awkward, meaning hard to handle or unpleasant. The outcome may not be what you want. The gifts you have could be beneficial to the whole world if used correctly.

So now that we are past the childhood stage let it be that, the past. There is nothing we can do about our childhood. Remember the past doesn't determine the future. The past only determines the present and the present determines the future. In other words, what we do today will determine where we are tomorrow. One cool thing about childhood is that the world is such a fascinating place when you are a child. I remember my father made it bigger than life. I recall my mom being the woman dreams were made of. My mom could make it all better, my older brothers were the coolest things since sliced bread.

Children develop lots of role models. Many people in my community were role models for me. If you look back on your childhood some of the people you looked up to are doing well and some are not. Keep in mind that no matter where you stand today there is someone that looks up to you. Someone that looks to you as a mentor. I define a mentor as a person or people who give you a tour of what to expect in life; that is someone tutoring you about life. In other words, a mentor is an individual that is able to assist you in looking at some of the outcomes before you actually experience the event. They are able to lead us through life's experiences based on what they have been through. My father was a tremendous mentor. Through his story telling and talking with me about life, he was able to give me a taste of his experiences, which in reality allowed me to experience it second hand. Kind of like second hand smoke, but with the opposite effect. People will look to you as a mentor particularly when you are going about doing the right thing. As you read this book, wherever you are in life, no matter what kind of person you are , today is a new day. You can be good. You can strive to be the best you can be. The best being "good". As you look back over your childhood, you can reflect on how you were spoken to as a child and see how that impacts how you speak to yourself as an adult. Determine how you are going to speak to yourself. It is your choice. You don't have to speak to yourself like you spoke to yourself as a child, or as you were spoken to as a child. Now as a teenager and an adult you can speak to yourself as a teenager and as an adult and use the words that you want to use. You can tell yourself, "I Want To Be Good".

Tools To Use

Each day that you wake up take time for yourself. Take thirty seconds to focus on all the positive qualities you own. If you find a day that you can not find the positive attributes, make some up for yourself. Your imagination can help you set up high expectations. Setting a goal is the first step in making dreams come true.

Relationships

---•---

CHAPTER 4

The scope of this book could not possibly reveal all of the aspects of relationships that people encounter on this earth. This chapter on relationships will be limited to two areas. This will give you the opportunity to develop a well thought out process in regard to relationships. Start to view yourself not as a body wandering through this world, but a mind that can lead you to the top of your mountain of success. Just think of how the people you hang around provide a springboard in your life. These people help determine the direction that you will go in as you come off your environmental springboard. As you dive there are many types of relationships that you will encounter throughout your life. Do not lose sight of you. The two aspects of relationships that I want you to focus on as you read are: 1) Relationships with friends and family and 2) Your relationship with yourself. These aspects of relationships involve emotions including happiness, joy, sadness, pity and many others. Relationships do not work by themselves as separate entities. They are dependent on each other. As you walk through life on your way to being good, you will walk with these relationships. How you respond will determine the person you become.

---•---

Relationships with friends and family

Your environment helps to determine how you think about yourself, how you think about others, and even how you feel about inanimate objects. Friends and family are part of your environment. Therefore the information they feed into your brain is processed and become the tools for your life's sculpture. Who you hang around with now will help determine who, what, and where you are tomorrow. This is part and partial of the elephant phenomenon.

When I was nine years old the basketball court in my hometown was on the corner of John Street and Clay Street. The basketball court was called the black top. The black top was the place to be. My friends and I would go to play ball even if we did not have a ball to play with. Most of the time people kept a ball in the corner of the black top. In the event a ball wasn't there we could always go across the street to Chris's house. He always had a ball. Chris would always complain, "Doggone, why don't you get your own ball," and then throw his ball out to us. At times we were without a ball. One day with no ball in the corner and Chris not home, we were silly out of luck. So, we were just kicking around rocks. Then my friend Jerry said, "Hey, can you touch this net?" There was a high rim and a low rim. The high rim was the regulation height of ten feet and the low rim which was for younger people was seven feet. I said, "I don't know. I never really tried". So Jerry went first and he didn't even touch the net. Then Eddie tried and he didn't touch the rim but he touched the net. Now it was my turn. I ran and jumped at the rim and touched the bottom of the rim. When I came down from that jump all my friends looked at me with amazement. They all said, "Man, you can really jump high." They started telling everybody at their schools, (we all went to different schools), that nobody could jump higher than Kenneth McKellar. I became known as the high jump king. Then people started saying that I could jump higher than anybody my age.

I started to believe this myself. Then anybody who went against me in jumping, I beat. Not only did I jump higher, I jumped much higher than any of my school friends. For the next two years I became known as the king of the leapers. Back then we used words like "ups." My friends said "McKellar has some serious ups." I still had ups when I got into the 6th grade. Now, in the 6th grade all the elementary schools came together under one roof called the middle school. I was in middle school with some of the best athletes in the area. People knew about my ups before I even got to the school. One day an older guy by the name of Wayne wanted to challenge me. He jumped first and he just missed the bottom of the net on a ten foot rim. I jumped and touched all of the net. Everyone went crazy and starting screaming, "Kenneth is the man, Kenneth is the man." I began to believe that I was the king of the jumpers. Any time I walked on the basketball court, my thinking was like that of an elevator. I was not coming down until I got to the top floor. Out jumping all my friends confirmed my greatness in my brain. As I was walking down the hall of John Witherspoon Middle School, I ran into Stephan Fletcher. Stephan was my best friend in all the world. Stimy (that is what we called Stephan) moved to North Carolina for two years when he was in the fourth grade. Now Stimy had recently moved back to the area. He was one of the best athletes that I had ever known. So, Stephan and I talked about what we could do and we were laughing. Stephan said, "I'm not a bad jumper but what I really do is run fast." He was the serious flash. When he would start running you couldn't see him. He was so fast he would almost turn invisible. One day during recess everyone was saying how high I could jump. So Stephan and I decided to see who could jump higher. Stephan jumped and he reached the bottom of the ten foot basket rim. I was astonished, I couldn't believe he was only in 6th grade and he could touch the bottom of the rim. I thought to myself okay if he can touch the bottom of the rim and I am the highest jumper around here I should be able to get up

"The only way you can act on the impossible is to know that you are worth all that life brings to you."

———————— • ————————

ALL I WANT TO BE
IS A GOOD MAN

over the rim. You see where your mind goes your body will follow. My mind said to my body, listen you are going to have to get up over the rim. I started running and my mind said to my feet, you are going to have to get up. I took another step and my mind said to my legs, you are going to have to get up. I took three more steps and just as I started to jump my mind spoke to my body. Get all of that body up there even that big butt. My mind led me up and I grabbed the rim. As I was swinging on the rim, I could hear the cheers of the playground. The recess aide blew his whistle, telling me not to hang on the rim. I swung three times on the rim then let go. When I came down everyone went crazy. Stimy was the first one to jump on me with congratulations. This was a great feeling. I went from grabbing the rim in the 6th grade to dunking the basketball in the 9th grade. I believe to this day that the jumping ability that I possessed throughout my school and college career was a direct result of what people thought about me when I was nine years old. Once I began believing in myself, gravity was merely a shackle on my legs for which I had the key. When I began believing in myself things really began to take form. I had the ability but I think I worked on it extra hard as a result of my environment. The people you hang around with now may help determine where and who you are tomorrow.

If you are hanging around negative people, chances are you will engage yourself in negative thinking. If you engage yourself in negative thinking your thought process turns negative, hence your actions turn negative. Remember, where your mind goes your body will follow. If you think you are worthy, that is worth the good in life, you will conduct yourself in the world to reach good possibilities. However, if you think that you are a worthless, that is worth less than everybody around you, then you will indulge yourself in self defeating behaviors. If you don't think you are worth two cents then those are the kind of relationships you are going to bid for--two cent relationships. But if you think you are a king, then you will walk like a king, talk like a king, you will become Mufasa. If you think of yourself as an awesome person then you will become just that. If the people you are hanging around with are going to help determine who you are and where you are going then you may want to choose your associates carefully. If the people you are hanging around are indulging in activities such as drugs, or guns, or violence or anything that you don't want to do, then it is time to disassociate yourself. If you don't know where you want to go or what you want to do with your life then stop reading right now and just sit and think, think about where you want to go and what you want to become. Be careful if you are riding the wave of the crowd because your destiny becomes determined by the movement of the crowd.

To be the person that you want to be, you may need to go against the current. Going against the current may require the paddles of a different relationship. To find the paddles of a different relationship you may need to wash the salt from your eyes for it may blind you to the support you seek to fight against the current of mediocracy. You have to remember that you were put on this earth destined for greatness as all humans are. However, few people follow Scott Peck and Take the Road Less Traveled. The few that choose the road to greatness and success in their personal happiness often seem to be traveling alone. When you are traveling in the nakedness of pursuing happiness you must choose your friends and associates wisely because these relationships will help clothe you in the armor of success. There are some people that take great pleasure in telling you that you cannot achieve your goals. They use phrases like, "Let me play devil's advocate." Now think about something that you want to do. Maybe you want to go to college. When you share this goal with a friend some will give you loving support. Others will take the opportunity to advocate for whom? The devil!!! They could advocate for anybody in the world but they chose to advocate for the devil. All the power the devil has he uses for the negative. Why do some people want to side with the devil? My thought is rather than advocating for the devil, hear me, and stand by my side this one time. Choose your friends carefully because your friends will help pick you up or help bring you down.

As I say, friends and relationships influence us. Don't misunderstand me. I am merely saying they are an aid in our thinking. They are not our thinking, nor are they responsible for the choices that we make. The choices that we make are our own. If you have people by your side, good friends, that are not going in the direction that you are going in, and are not helping you become the person you want to be, you may have to pull away from those friends. Yes, life may knock you down but you have the ability to get back up. Life may throw you a curve and strike you out, but you still have the choice to step up to the plate. Be the person that you are inspired to be and walk to the beat of your drum. Will you be led astray or will you lead others? Make every attempt you can to surround yourself with the people that you aspire to be like or with people that are doing the things that you want to do, and with the people that have walked the path that you have chosen. When you place yourself with people you choose to be like, two things happen. One, you can start to develop a mental image of what you are to become. Second, the people you associate yourself with help to direct your thoughts.

Relationships with yourself

What kind of person do you want to be? When you wake up in the morning and look at yourself in the mirror what kind of person do you want to see? Yes, your childhood and your environment greatly influence who you are and what you are going to become. But, they by no means make the final determination of who you are. You determine who you are. Do you sell yourself short and then become upset because you fall short of your goals? How you feel about yourself has a direct impact on how people feel about you. The key is to establish who you want to be and who you feel comfortable being. Don't let anybody bring you down. Don't let anybody shatter your dreams because of what they think about you. What people say and think about you is none of your concern. You don't have to worry about that. The key is to decide who and where you want to be. Walk to the beat of your dream.

The big step in developing a relationship with yourself is taking responsibility for yourself. Decide that whatever happens in your life you are responsible. Now you have the power to dictate your destiny. With responsibility in your hands, you have the power to build the life that you want.

"Once you become focused on your goals you can't beat a good man." My father used to say that to me all the time. I had to work really hard in high school. I was pulling all nighters in high school to pull B's. At the beginning of my junior year my guidance counselor called me in and said, "Listen, Ken I think that you should spend another year in high school." I said, "But I have worked hard, I have all the classes I need so far, in fact I am two classes ahead of where I need to be. I am right on plan to graduate. Why would I want to stay in high school another year? I want to go to college." She said, "You can't go to college." I said, "Why not?" She replied, "Because special education kids don't go to college". I said, "I didn't know that, so I can't go to college?" She said, "No, you will never make it in college." I said, "But I want to get my Ph.D. in psychology," and she said, "But you can't do that because special ed people don't go to college. A Ph.D. would require college. I think you should spend another year in high school".

Now, I had been doing everything I could to ensure that I would graduate, I was good, and my father said that you can't beat a good man. I felt I was a good man, or a least a good boy trying to become a man. Now the counselor was telling me that all my hard work was going to lead me to an additional year of high school. That was absurd. All my friends were graduating. It was at that time in my life that I realized that you can beat a good man if he doesn't believe in himself. You can beat any good athlete if he doesn't believe in himself. You can beat any perspective competitor for a promotion or a job if he doesn't believe in himself. Believing in yourself is a component of being good. So, if you are good and you believe in yourself you can't be beaten.

I walked out of that guidance counselor's office thinking that college was not an option for me. I believed that I was a good man, and I always thought I could go to college. Now, I didn't think it was an option for me. We must educate ourselves. Education is knowledge and knowledge is power. When you have the power of knowledge you have the power to control your life. Needless to say I went through my junior year thinking that college was not an option for me. The next year at the beginning of the year, I reported again to my guidance counselor. When I walked into her office she said, "I don't handle the M's (as in McKellar) anymore, you will need to see Mr. Trotman". I went to see Mr. Trotman and the first thing he said is, "Well, what do you want to do with your life?" I said, "I really don't know, I wanted to go to college." Mr. Trotman stopped me dead and said, "So, why aren't you going?" I said, "Because I am in special education and I can't. Didn't you read that big book in there with my educational history?" Trotman responded: "Wait a minute, who told you this?" Before I could answer he said, "Never mind. Let me tell you something. *You can do anything you want to do.*"

Mr. Trotman's words changed my academic life. He said, "College is just hard work and determination. If you are willing to put in the hard work and are determined to go after what you want and believe that you can get the grade, go. You deserve to go to college. The only thing between you and your college degree is time." He then told me the story about the Wright brothers. Orville and Wilbur

"Your thoughts are the gym of your mind. Now I ask, what kind of shape are you in?"

—————————•—————————

ALL I WANT TO BE
IS A GOOD MAN

Wright owned a bicycle shop in Dayton, Ohio. After hearing about flight by hot air balloons and gliders they decided they wanted to fly an aircraft heavier than air powered by an engine. After many unsuccessful attempts at flight the brothers finally met with success. On December 17, 1903 in Kitty Hawk, North Carolina the first engine powered air craft flew for 12 seconds and covered a distance of 120 feet. These twelve seconds changed the thinking of the world and established a new belief.

After telling the story about the Wright brothers, Mr. Trotman said, "Now what is it that you want to do with your life?" I joked, "I want to be a pilot." It was an exciting story. Mr. Trotman reopened my eyes to the possibility that I could go to college. I believed in myself. Because I believed in myself, I graduated high school. Because I graduated from high school I applied to college. Because I applied to college I was accepted. Because I was accepted I worked hard. Because I worked hard in college and believed in myself I graduated from West Virginia University. Because I graduated I applied to Hood College Graduate School. Because I applied and believed in myself I got accepted and because I got accepted I went. Because I worked hard and believed in myself I got my Masters Degree. I am not done yet, I am going after my doctorate.

As you build your relationship with yourself, determine who you want to be and what you want out of your life and do not stop until you get it. Don't give up, don't give in, don't let down. Slow down if you must, let down some if you have to, bend if it helps, but as Winston Churchill said, **never, never, never give in.** When you start building a relationship with yourself you can become excited about who you are and where you want to be.

TOOLS TO USE

1.   Write down what you want out of life.   Make sure the people that are surrounding you are supportive.

2.   The best way to hit the target is to see it first.   Then shoot till you hit the bullseye.   What is your goal?

Excitement

CHAPTER 5

I have three sons, ages five, three, and two. My boys run every-where. I am talking about low down flat out running. They sprint everywhere they go. They run outside. They run inside, upstairs and downstairs. They run to the bathroom. (Why do boys wait until the last minute before they go to the bathroom?) They run out of the bathroom and run to the playground. They run everywhere except to bed. There was a time when I would exhaust my energy and waste my breath saying slow down, stop, not to fast, stop, stop, stop. But, the boys were on the move and moving fast. Then I realized they are just excited about everything they do. It is exciting to go outside, it is exciting to go upstairs, to get in the car. Everything excites them. When the boys are in that excited state they become intrigued and just have to be there. In fact, being there becomes the goal. Not only do they have to be there, they have to get there as fast as they can. The little mites play as hard as they can play to get the most out of the pre-sent event. They put all the energy they have into whatever they are doing. The boys get so excited and focused, I think they forget to run out of energy. One day, I was leaning up against an oak tree with a rake in one hand and a pair of scissors that I had taken away from Kevin (my middle son) in the other hand. I was looking at my three

●

sons run around with all this excitement. I was thinking to myself, "if I had half that excitement about life, things would get done." Then I started thinking about excitement. There are many words that mean excitement such as passion, fervor, moved, worked up, inspired, aroused, stimulated, motivated, provoked, spurred, impelled, incited, inflamed, initiated, kindled, and egged on. These are just a few of the words that come to mind when I think of excitement. I can see this in my boys as they are always moving. They are always moving. The boys spend more time doing what needs to be done in their play world. Little Stephen does not think about doing. Kevin spends his days in the act of his pursuit. Jonathan spends his days in the emotional moment. What can we learn from the McKellar boys? As I look at my offspring I note that they rarely get stuck getting ready to do. The boys just do. At times we as adults spend a lifetime getting ready to go after our dreams. The only thing that slows the boys down are adults telling them to hold on a minute.

Now, the quick ambitions of the boys do not always work for their Dad. They are inspired. *Excitement* is contagious! When one person starts to get excited about something it is contagious. As I was hanging out with my boys I felt myself getting more and more excited. I had to decide what excitement meant to me. To me this was focusing on what I wanted to do in life. This is excitement.

There are things in life that we encounter on a day to day basis. Hardships that life presents to us. There are also positive things that life just hands to us. These are few and far between. In the middle is a huge space of neutral area that is labeled neither positive or negative. This space allows you to determine whether the cup is half full or half empty. With every adversity, if you can learn to look for the positive, you are making steps to becoming good. Thomas Edison blew up ten thousand light bulbs in his quest to make the first incandescent light. He was also able to look at each failed trial as a success because he was closer to finding the perfect light bulb. The Wright

●

brothers found many different ways that a plane would not fly before they took their first successful flight in 1907. Michael Jordan was cut from his high school basketball team before he became Air Jordan. He watched his high school teammates play many games of basketball while he sat on the bench. Scottie Pippen was the equipment manager on his college team before he went on to become a four time NBA champion and member of the Olympic Dream Team. Sidney Portier was kicked out of acting school and later became the first African-American male actor to win a Grammy for best actor.

Bill Cosby quit high school, got his GED, joined the army, and had many unsuccessful shows before he went on to earn a Ph.D., or play the part of Heathcliff Huxtable. He was the first Black male to co-star in a television series fifteen years before hitting number one with the Cosby Show.

What did all these people have in common? They are seen as successful people. The main attribute they had in common was that they set their sights on what they thought they were meant to do. You can achieve by practicing and focusing on what it is that you want to achieve. I once heard a song that said if you want to be somebody and go somewhere you better wake up and smell the coffee. You can't get where you want to go without moving, physically or mentally. One of the greatest gifts that humans beings were given is excitement. When you get excited about something movement takes place and when you move the people around you move. When the people around you move they build energy and energy builds excitement. Start to put a little pep in your step and walk a little faster towards your dreams. A good person helps bring people up not put people down. As you move a little faster get excited about who you want to be and where you are going. As you move forward in life you radiate excitement to those around you. As you spread your passion around, excitement radiates back to you. How do you keep this excitement alive in your life? I think my oldest son, five-year-old Jon, said it best when he said "Why can't we." Jon is one of those kind of kids, who no matter what happens, says, "Why can't we." I could come into the house and say we can't go to the store because the car blew up and Jon would say, "Why can't we walk to the store?" Then I would say, "Jon because I don't have any money," and he would interject, "Well just go to the machine and get money." I would say, "Jon, because I don't have any money in the bank," and then he would say, "Just use your card and get some money." Jon is under the impression that anything could happen. He will come in the house and say, "Dad I want a toy." If I reply, "Well you can't buy a toy." he will reply, "Why not?" If I say, "Because I don't have any money," he will say, "Why can't we ask the neighbors for money?" Hearing Jon say, why can't, why can't, why can't, over and over again I began to think this way also. I began to say, "Why can't we make it happen? What can we do to make it happen? What is the positive in this? What is the good in this? How can I make it better?" It is important to focus on what we can do, rather then what we can not. This way you can focus on making any situation better!!!

Another way to keep yourself excited is to give yourself a verbal massage at least twice a day. A verbal massage is talking to yourself. Start your verbal massage with your mission statement. Do this by establishing what you are going to accomplish today and how you are going to accomplish it. Say every positive thing you can to yourself. Think about what you plan to do with yourself and the time frame you have chosen. Keep in mind that this day, this minute, this hour, this second is all the time you have. You have lost the time that has passed and you do not own the time that is ahead. You can not bank on time, and you can not get a loan on the future. The only thing that is guaranteed is what you have right now. The maturity of your loan on the future is determined by your work ethic today. Excitement brings productive work habits. Be excited, talk to yourself, tell yourself how good you are and that you can accomplish your goals.

*"No way Jon,
the elephants
could just break
the string and
come up here and
eat all of us."*

———————— ● ————————

Exercise Excitment!

TOOLS TO USE

1) Start now. Do the small things that will move you towards your goals.

2) There are no small things when moving towards your dreams. It's all huge!

Aspirations

●

CHAPTER 6

One of my biggest aspirations in life is to get my doctorate. Ever since I was about fifteen-years-old, I knew exactly what I wanted to do with my life. I wanted to work with kids and their families as a therapist. The aspiration of working with kids came true for me. As I started my work career one of my first jobs allowed me to see the positive effect and change that a good therapist could have on people. This job was a Family Services Coordinator for a home based counseling service. I worked for a private firm and the bulk of my job was going from home to home working with families. This kept the child out of a residential facility and in the home with the family. It was the first therapeutic position I had. It was very challenging, as I usually visited four to six families a day. I was spending a huge amount of time on the road by myself. As I traveled back and forth, I used to daydream about all of the things that I wanted out of life. I had tremendous aspirations. I wanted to get more education and get my doctorate. I wanted to become a therapist. Once a week the group of Family Service Coordinators would get together and have a meeting and dialogue back and forth about their cases. After the meeting I would often sit around and talk to some of the other counselors. This was a young crew. I was twenty-three years old at that time and

●

37

my colleagues were about the same age. Two of my colleagues and I generally went out to lunch once a week and sat around and talked about what we hoped to do in the years to come. I would sit down and tell my colleagues that I wanted to get my Master's degree and then my Doctorate because I wanted to be a therapist working in a school. Not just a therapist but, a good therapist. The kind of *good* that my Dad talked about. A therapist that could actually empower people. I want to help them, create the change that they want in life.

I was a dreamer. Not only did I want to be a good therapist, I wanted to be the best motivational speaker on the planet. I wanted to make change on a one-to-one level as well as touch many people at one time. As a speaker, I dreamed of making a tape, in fact two tapes. I was dreaming in detail and telling my colleagues the McKellar plan. My thoughts were to call the first tape YOU ARE THE VEHICLE TO YOUR DESTINY and it would let people know that they are the ones that are going to get them where they want to go. My next tape would be a tape catered to younger kids called Where Your Mind Goes Your Body Will Follow and it would be a tape of stories. I explained this in detail to my colleagues. I was a dreamer. I would tell them my dreams and they would just look at me with a blank look. I would continue, I want to write a book, maybe two books. The dream did not stop there. I also want to write a play called THE MIGHTY STRUGGLE and that would be an in-depth look at adolescence. A one man play performed by yours truly. Oh no, the dream did not stop there. My biggest project, a movie. I am going to write and star in a movie called The Magic Chair. By now they were looking at each other and shaking their heads. I think they wanted to put me in a home off in the woods. This way my crazy thoughts could not get me hurt. One of my colleagues even said, "You are just a dreamer Kenneth. That is all you will ever be - a dreamer that spends his life outside this world" Then another colleague looked at her and said, "But he sure does dream big." They were both right about me. I am a dreamer and I do dream big. I think of myself as a blue collar dreamer. I am a blue collar dreamer, because I dream hard around the clock. It is important to dream because everything in our man made existence started out with a dream, an idea, an aspiration. The chair you are sitting in started out as an idea. Chairs just didn't pop onto the face of the earth. The cars that you drive started out with a dream. Carl Benz invented the first four stroke gasoline car engine. An invention that eventually lead to the development of the car that he would later name after his wife. This car was the Mercedes Benz. **DREAM ON**. Dream big. Dreams are what goals are made of. A dream is merely a goal with an expiration date. You can set you goals based off of your dreams and set a date for the dream to become a reality. Then you have actually made the first step in accomplishing something. As my colleagues were talking to me they started playing devil's advocate. They wanted me to know all of the reasons I could not accomplish my goals. I couldn't get my Doctorate because I wasn't smart enough. I couldn't be a professional speaker because no one would listen. I couldn't write a book because my spelling was atrocious (they used words like this). This was my work friends helping me out. I could not make a tape because my big butt would not fit in the studio. My guess is that the play and the movie were so far off they were not worth mentioning. You will have people that will make it their business to tell you what you can't do. They will go out of their way to help you out of your dreams. They will let you know what you can't do. There are people that love to cater to this cancerous stagnating disability called *limitations.* People will go out of their way to limit your dreams and aspirations.

Do not let anybody talk you out of your dreams. Don't let anyone talk you out of what you want to achieve. Just believe. Believe in yourself and believe in your dream. Dreams take time and effort. You may fail in reaching your aspirations but use these failures as stepping stones not stumbling blocks. Even when it doesn't work out right, hold on tight. Hold on tight to your dreams.

The first thing you want to do when you start to dream big is dream about it over and over again. Immerse yourself in thought about what you want out of life. Begin to hang around positive people. When I started to live my dream the second thing I did was quit that job. I got away from the limiting thinking of my co-workers. I enrolled at Hood College to start working on my Master's Degree as well as my dream. I also had aligned myself with more positive and affirming people. I didn't even know how powerful different people could be. I started working at Pathways Schools. Pathways was a program which worked with kids and helped them address the problems of life, natural adolescent life, community life, and life problems particular to their situation. The people that I became associated with there were very positive and upbeat people. I realized these were the kind of people that I needed and wanted to be around me. This was a job I had wanted to do since I was fifteen-years-old. I was realizing my dream.

I went on to receive my Masters from Hood. Getting my Master's was a significant step for me, for it gave me more confidence. The next step was to do educational speaking and before too long I was giving motivational speeches to children. Soon, I had a tape out. Now I am writing a book, I WANT TO BE GOOD. While I was driving to work every day with the music blasting and thinking about being a speaker, writing a book, or doing a play, it just seemed so far away. What kept me going was something my father said to me when I was younger. I didn't even understand it at first, in fact I didn't understand until I was sitting at my desk at Pathways Schools after a long exhausting day realizing that I was doing what I dreamed of.

I thought back to when I was in elementary school. My dad and I were walking around the park at my school. Dad was a school aide. He was escorting me to class. (Dad was coming to school so much to check on my brothers and me, the principal offered him a job.)

Suddenly, we both just stopped and looked at this butterfly resting on the playground slide. This was the most beautiful butterfly I had ever seen. I was a hard rock kid and I had never really stopped to smell the roses. For some reason this butterfly caught the attention of us both. We stood in silence and looked at this beautiful butterfly. I just looked, enjoying these few seconds with my Dad before I returned to my 5th grade academic regimen. My father said, "Just think before that butterfly made the transition into such a beautiful creature it was a caterpillar." As I look back on those words, I figure my Dad spoke of the struggle leading to GOOD.

Hold tight to your dreams. As you struggle along the highway with the thoughts of flying with the beauty of success, crawl with a rigid determination that no one will stop you. Don't let anyone's weight tie you down from your flight of beauty, the flight of dreams and your aspirations.

How do you start to act on your dreams? There are five steps. The first one is to write them down. What is it that you want to do? What is it that you dream about doing? Write it down. Write it down in detail. The second step is to become a dream planner. Make a plan of exactly how you want to get to your destiny. If your dream is to go to college write down exactly what you need and how you are going to get there. For instance, do you need a certain grade point average? What college do you want to go to? What financial backing do you need to go to college? How do you get that financial backing? Start making a plan of exactly how you are going to reach that dream. Become a dream planner. Third, make each day count. Stay in focus and concentrate on your plan. Lots of times what happens is we get off track. Stay on track with your goal each day. Stay busy with your plan. Do something everyday that will bring you closer to what you want out of life. Make each day count. The fourth step is to do the little things. I was talking to my brother, Keith, who is a personal trainer. I was telling him that I wanted to get strong, really strong. He looked at me and said, "Well I see you have been working on your large muscles. That is good, however if you want to get strong you have to work on your smaller muscles too. As your smaller muscles get stronger they help your larger muscles, so that your whole body is getting stronger". Do the little things. Fifth, associate yourself with a positive context everyday. Whether it is a friend that is a positive person that you can talk with, or a motivational tape that you can listen to, or a book that is informational and positive. Everyday associate yourself with something of a positive context.

These are the five TOOLS TO USE that can be a springboard to making your dreams come true. These five TOOLS will spring you into the next level.

Transformation

C H A P T E R   7

My three year old son, Kevin, has always liked sitting down watching sports events with me. One aftenoon we were watching Michael Jordan and the Chicago Bulls take on Shaquille O'Neal and the Orlando Magic. Halfway through the game the Bulls were winning. Jordan was having one of his fantastic shooting days. A NIKE commercial came on that ended with the words JUST DO IT. Kevin said, "Dad what does that say?" and I said, "Just do it." Kevin said, "Do what?", and I said, "Do whatever it is that you want to do." He said, "What do I want to do?" I said, "I don't know, but whatever you want to do that commercial says go ahead and do it." Go ahead and start now. (Kevin, you did not understand it at that time. Now as you and others read this book, my hope is that you do understand what NIKE was saying and just do it.) Do whatever it is that you want to do, start now. Make that transformation from whatever you have in your brain as a fantasy to putting it into tangible forms. Make it a reality. In other words, embark on your own metamorphosis no matter what your present situation. Like the butterfly make the change that will enhance your beauty. If you want to make an athletic team and get cut, just do it. Just do whatever you need to do to make it next year. If you want to go to college and you don't have the money, just do it.

Find out ways to get the money. Find out how you can get the financial backing. Just do it. If you just started a new job, and you see another position that is a promotion that you want, just do it. Do whatever you need to do to get the promotion. Do you need to work late? Then stay late. Do you need to work harder, do you need more education? JUST DO IT. Who is that girl walking down the street fine as can be? Is that your future mate, is that who you want to date ? Just do it, go ahead and ask her out and see what happens. Transform those thoughts and fantasies into realities. JUST DO IT.

How do you start making that transformation? My first thought is that you want to start thinking and acting in accordance with what you want to become. In other words, whatever it is that you want to do think about how that person thinks. If you want to be straight a A student start thinking like a straight A student and start acting like a straight A student. If a straight A student takes home extra homework then you might take home extra homework. If a straight A student stays after school and asks the teacher for extra work, then you ask the teacher for extra work. Your grades will eventually get better. Where your mind goes your body will follow. The you that you see in your mind's eye, is the you that will carry your brain. So, if you are thinking about your dream and walking in accordance to your dream then eventually you will start to live your dream. My father used to say to me, "Even a fool can sit with kings until he opens his mouth." Now, my father would throw verbiage out like that all the time. This tended to leave me in the shadows of thought. When I was a little kid I thought to myself, what is he talking about? By the time I got in high school when my Dad left me with a thought to ponder. I thought to myself what is this man saying? Then, when I got in college I found myself saying more times than not, doggone, I go to school and Dad gets smarter. What I guess he meant by even a fool can sit with kings until he opens up his mouth is that if I look at the king with my mouth shut I can see how he walks, how he talks, and see the things that he has done to become a king. After I have learned kingly ways my mouth will open with knowledge. Start to make your transformation. First, start thinking and acting in accordance with your dreams. Second, talk to people who are doing or have done what you are trying to do. That goes back to the king analogy. If you start hanging around with people who have already accomplished your goal it will open a mental door in your brain that says he did it. This makes it possible for me to reach the goal. You can see and touch and realize that they put on their pants the same way that you do, just one leg at a time. But as you are talking to them, be careful of their advice and know that the way they have accomplished their success may not be the same way you will need to succeed. The steps that you need to take may be different. The most important thing that you can take from this role model is that it is possible or that it can happen. If it can happen for him, it can happen for you. Talk to people who are doing or have done what you want to do.

Third, find out what has been done in your dream of choice and go a step further. As you are talking to people go a step further. As you are talking to people find out what they have done to achieve their accomplishments and go a step further. Do more than what is expected of you. My mother is a prime example of an individual who constantly and consistently would go the extra step and always did more than what was expected of her. As a mother and as a wife she always left with her family saying "Mom that was good." She would leave us in awe of how much she could accomplish in one day. She was able to accomplish the tasks that she did and take care of four knuckle headed boys plus the author of this book. Find out what needs to be done to accomplish your dream of choice and go the extra mile.

When you are looking for whatever it is that you want to become in life transform yourself into a good person. You were put on this planet for a reason and you were put on this planet to achieve.

Start with the good in you. The transformation will come with good as defined at the start of this book. So rid yourself of the negativity and look at the positive. No matter how bleak it may seem, just do it. Become incessant with your dream. Become incessant with you and the good in you.

Incessant

·

CHAPTER 8

In the early 1950's there was a boy named L.P.. He grew up in Lumberton, North Carolina in a neighborhood called Tin Top Alley. Tin Top Alley was several houses seated next to each other in a "U" shape. There must have been sixteen or seventeen cottage type houses in this area. The reason it was called Tin Top Alley was because all of the white houses in this U-shape arena had red tin roofs. When it rained you could hear the rain ping on the tin roofs. This made for great night time sleep music. L.P. grew up in a three room home where he lived with his younger brother Charles, his two younger sisters Shirley and Sheby, and his mother and father. His father was in the service and was only home during times of extended leave. Tin Top Alley was like many housing areas in the South where the families bonded together to become one large family unit. So, not only did Mr. Gilmore discipline you, so did Ms. Kitty Bell, and Miss Terri Tugball and any of the other adults. L.P. learned many of his athletics and antics in Tin Top Alley. The courtyard formed by this U-shaped band of houses served as an activity arena. So, whatever sport was in season was played in this area. It acted as the football field, the baseball field, the basketball court, the kickball field, the hide and seek pole, and the kick the can court. As the children of Tin Top Alley grew up it also became the courting arena

·

where couples could hold hands as they walked around. They were duly supervised by the arena spectators looking through the windows or sitting on the front porches. L.P. grew up in Tin Top Alley and it was a huge part of his childhood thinking. When L.P. was in 8th grade he decided that when he began attending high school he would play football. Now, there are two things wrong with this picture. One, no one from Tin Top Alley had ever played football on the high school team before. The second was that no freshman in the history of J.C. Hayward High School had played on the varsity football team. There was no junior varsity team. There was no freshman team, only a varsity team. If you made the team, you played on the varsity team. No freshman had ever tried out for the varsity team. At the end of his 8th grade year the 119 pound L.P. set his sight on the J.C. Hayward High School football team.

L.P. told his friends that he wanted to play football. They said things like, "Are you crazy, are you an idiot, you can't play football. No one from Tin Top Alley has ever been on the team, and no freshman has ever even tried out. What makes you think you can do that?" But L.P. was incessant in his thinking and the more people told him he could not play the more determined he was to play. That was all he said to himself and to other people. People would sit around the courtyard saying, "Did you hear about what L.P. wants to do? He wants to play football. Those other men will kill him. Somebody better talk to that boy. Let me play devil's advocate L.P.," is how they started. They would say, "L.P. you can't play football." L.P. always replied, "I want to play football." This went on and on. L.P. started to prepare himself both mentally and physically. He started to run, do push ups, and carry around cinder blocks (he didn't have weights to lift). He did pushups with his sisters on his back and he did sit ups with his brother Charles holding his legs and pushing him down. He went to his mother and told her that he wanted to play football. His mom looked at him and said, "I don't know." L.P. persisted. His father was of course away in the service so his mother wrote his father a letter asking his father's permission. His father sent him a letter telling him that he could play and he sent him an athletic bag from Germany as well as some football cleats. His mother gave him these things and said, "Your father said you could play. Now don't mess up this bag and these cleats. You take good care of them". So L.P., who was ecstatic, ran out the door, running his usual get in shape mileage. He proceeded with his all consuming training throughout the summer. He was the talk of Tin Top Alley. People would even come up to his mother and say, "are you really going to let that boy play football?"

The thinking was that he would not last long. No one from Tin Top Alley had ever played on the team. No freshman had never tried out for the team much less made the team. L.P had a belief in himself that was incredible. He had a fire shut up in his bones that he could no longer contain. L.P was incessant in his thinking. I want to play football, I want to play football was his moving chant. He changed his body from a boyish figure to a well tuned 165 pound football machine. He was small, but he was stronger and faster then ever before. He was in top football shape. Mid-August came and it was time for football practice. L.P. grabbed his bag and packed his shirt, his jock strap, his socks, his shoes, and his towel and walked to the bus stop. As he was waiting he was very much aware that he was the youngest person at the bus stop. Nobody was paying much attention to him. During those times when the bus came it was not driven by an adult bus driver. A senior student drove the bus. Seniors were considered adults, juniors close to it, sophomore were want-to-be adults, and freshmen were nobodies. L.P. was a nobody hanging around adults who were smoking fresh cigars made right from the tobacco fields. They would come to practice after working in the tobacco fields. L.P. was waiting at the bus stop while the "adults" (upper-classmen) were having a great time ignoring him, and the bus pulled up. Everyone piled on the bus. The bus pulled off and L.P. took a seat in a middle row of the bus. This big upper class man, six foot six inches tall and weighing 275 pounds approached L.P. and said, "Where are you going little fella?" L.P. looked at the upper class man called Bubba Jackson and said, "I want to play football, I want to play football." Bubba said, "Open up the doors," as someone opened up the back door of the bus, Bubba picked L.P. up by his collar and his pants belt and threw him off the bus. As the bus pulled away they threw his bag out to him saying, "And take this raggedy bag with you." They all laughed as they drove off to practice. L.P. had been talking about playing football for the last month and a half. His dad had bought him new football shoes and a bag so he couldn't go home. He went to town and looked around the stores until it was time for football practice to be over, then walked home. When he got home his mother said, "How did practice go?" L.P. replied, "It went all right. It was almost as if I wasn't even there." His mother said, "Are they giving you a hard time?" L.P said, "No, they are doing all right by me". His brother Charles would say, "L.P., you are the man, you are the man, you are the man aren't you L.P.?" L.P would answer, "Well, we will see, things are just starting. This is only the first day." The next day L.P. went to the bus stop and waited for the bus to come. The upper class men went on about their business talking and acted as if he wasn't there. Then the bus came and everybody got on. The bus pulled off and then Big Bubba Jackson stopped the bus, grabbed L.P. and threw him off again. L.P. walked around town. The next morning the same thing happened. L.P went to the bus stop. They acted like he wasn't there. Everybody got on the bus and Big Bubba Jackson signaled the guys to open up the back door and they threw him off the bus. This took place for the next several days. They would throw L.P. off the bus and he would go walk around town until football prac-tice was over and he could go home. It became a joke. The other play-ers would see L.P. coming and start laughing. They would say, this guy just doesn't give up. After a week of this the only bruises from playing football that he had to show were bruises of cinders embedded in the palm of his hand and the scrape on his knee. He had seen no football action what so ever. After ten days of being thrown off the bus, he approached the bus stop again. The same ritual took place. The players ignored him and acted as if he wasn't there. The bus came and they all piled on. Bubba was ready to throw L.P. off the bus when the six foot six inch 263 pound lineman Charlie Brown stood up and said, "Let him stay. When he comes to practice we will kill him." Then he looked at L.P. and said, "You want to play football? L.P said, "I want to play football, I want to play football." Charlie Brown said, "Have fun today because it will be your last". So L.P. made the half hour ride to the football field. He got off the bus, put on his equipment and did the warm up drills. Then it came time to scrimmage. The coach said, "Hey you, young man what is your name?" The young man replied, "L.P." "I want you to go out there and play outside linebacker." L.P. said, "okay" and sprinted to the outside linebacker position. The boys on the football team tried to kill L.P. They stepped on him, they kicked him, they spit on him, they punched him, they twisted his arm, they twisted his leg, they kneed him in the back, they elbowed him in the head. They tried to kill him but after every play he would get up and stumble back to the huddle thinking to himself, I want to play football. After practice the others said, "I bet he won't be back tomorrow." L.P. barely made it home. His brother Charles and his sister Shirley met him at the corner of their unpaved street and saw him stumbling toward the house and helped him home. His mother said, "What happened to you?" He grunted, "I played football." She cried, "I don't want you to go back out there." He pleaded, "You and Dad said I could play." She said, "Boy, I just can't see you get hurt." So, his brother and sister iced him down, and bandaged him up and got him ready for the next day. The next day L.P. was back at the bus stop. As he walked to the bus stop the fellas giggled and said, "What is he doing back here?" He got on the bus and rode the half hour to the football field and they tried to kill him again with the same antics. That afternoon his brother Charles and his sister Shirley met him at the bus stop and escorted him home. He barely made it home, just lying down in the middle of the floor. They massaged him, and iced him down and got him ready for practice again. Mind you this was just practice. It wasn't even game time yet. L.P. went back to the bus stop, with fire in his heart, to play football. They said, "You have fun today L.P. because you will not be back tomorrow." He got to practice and his coach said, "Hey you, L.P. come here. Did you ever run the football before?" L.P. said "No." but the coach said, "Get over there you are going to be my fullback." Every time they gave L.P. the ball all thirteen men would tackle him. Now, I know those of you who follow football are saying, but there are only eleven players. I am telling you, some of the trainers would jump in because L.P. was a freshman and he wasn't sup-posed to be on the field. Not only was he not supposed to be out there, he wasn't supposed to out play the upper classmen. So they tried to kill him. I am not kidding, the upperclassmen wanted to bring death to this freshman because they wanted to bring death to the idea of a freshman playing and hanging out with these grown men. In their minds he had not completed his rites of passage into adulthood or earned the honor of playing football on the J.C. Hayward football team. Once again after practice he was met by his brother and his sister and as they escorted him home L.P. noticed something different as he entered the arena of Tin Top Alley. All his friends and neighbors were outside greeting him and asking him how we was feeling, and how football was going and cheering him on. They were patting him on the back and asking if they could hold his bag or walk him home. He started to become a celebri-ty in Tin Top Alley. This support given to him by his peers only encour-aged L.P.. He got up the next morning and looked in the mirror and gave himself what I call today, a verbal massage. He said to himself, "I am going to play football, I am going to play football." He walked to the bus stop and this time when they saw him coming they stood in com-plete silence. Nobody uttered a word. They just eyed him as if to say, "I can't believe he is back. This fool really wants to play football." (You see when you go after your goal hard enough even your enemies start to secretly cheer for you. You can not keep a good man down.) So the rest of the practices continued until J.C. Hayward scrimmaged another team from across town. When L.P. played against the other team he ran all over his opponents. He kicked them, he punched them, he stepped on them, he stood out. When he walked away he was incessant. He was going to play football and no one was going to stand in his way. The pain that marinated in his bones didn't deter him. The fear that kindled in his heart was quickly extinguished and replaced with the fire of relentlessness. L.P. wanted to play football. He was unstoppable. Relentless and tenacious his mission, to play football. His statement, "I want to play football."

L.P. McKellar, my father, demonstrated to me this incessant attitude; this obsession that you must define inside yourself who you want to be so you can achieve. Not only did L.P. start on the J.C. Hayward High School team as a freshman, he started on the team all four years of high school. In L.P.'s senior year he was captain of his football team.

L.P. wanted to play football. What is it that you want out of life? What is it that you want to do? I always wondered how he could start on both offense and defense, meaning he was always one of the twenty-two people on the field all of the time. He played more than many of the upper class men and was respected by the upper class men. He became a celebrated hero in Tin Top Alley. I said, "Dad how is it that you were able to do so well against your opponents?" He looked at me and said, "There was nothing that my opponents could do to me that my teammates had not already done." The only obstacle that you should allow to stop you from reaching your goal is the obstacle of death. If you are still breathing, it is still possible, and if it is still possible, it is likely that you can make it happen. Being incessant means that you have to go for it and do whatever is necessary. Do whatever it takes to get what you want. When you are at that point, when you are willing to do what ever it takes, short of hurting someone else, then you will reach your goals. Be obsessed with your goals.

Be incessant.

"How do you stay obsessed and incessant?" First, do it one more time, until you reach your goal. If you fall down, do it one more time. If you fail, do it one more time. If it doesn't work out do it one more time until it does. Do not stop. Second, practice what you want to be good at. If you want to be good at math, then practice, and practice, and practice some more. Practice does not make perfect. Practice will bring you closer to your goal. Third, set your goals high and put a time limit on it. If you do not reach the goal within the time limit, give yourself an extension. You are what you aspire to be.

Vehicle

———————————————— • ————————————————

C H A P T E R   9

Go after what you want to be in life because you are the vehicle to your destiny. You are what powers you. You can mold yourself into the you that you want to be. Start to focus in your mind and crystallize your definition of good and what that means to you. Don't ever lose sight of the fact that you are going to get you where you want to go. Plain and simple, you are the vehicle to your destiny. The road you travel is controlled by your mental steering wheel. Being the vehicle to your destiny means you have a unique automobile. It is not like Henry Ford's invention. This is not like Carl Benz' creation. You are made by a creator outside of this earth. Your engine is like no other. No one can ever actually drive your vehicle. No one can get into you and direct you. However, you will have people who sit in the back-seat. People that will attempt to direct you from the side of the road. You will have people that will sit in the passenger seat next to you and tell you what you ought to be doing. Whether you choose to listen to these voices or acknowledge the gestures, you are the vehicle. You can choose to respond or not to respond. As you travel on the road to where you want to be you will run into many potholes, and even road closings. You may need to take detours in order to reach your destiny. You are the vehicle to your destiny. As you travel

————————————————— • —————————————————

"Take a glimpse of what you are and what you can be."

---•---

I WANT TO
BE GOOD

on the road to your destiny keep in mind that it does not matter where you think you are as much as it matters where you think you are going. You are the vehicle to your destiny, you are the engine, the thinking that powers you. Basically the responsibility of the body of the car is to carry the engine. I feel this holds true for you; your body is responsible for holding your engine, your brain. You are the vehicle to your destiny. You are the headlights. You can focus on a goal and go after it. You are the brakes, so you can stop yourself from reaching a goal, or reading another page in this book. You can stop yourself from going to another class, or from filling out another job or school application. You can stop yourself. But don't! You are also the gas pedal so you can push down to give yourself more fuel to light your fire. You can educate yourself and get to college or to a trade school. You can fuel your engine in regard to the next step you want to take in life. What will take you closer to who you want to be? You can turn left over the horizon if you feel as though a left turn will take you closer to what you want out of life, or you can follow Scott Peck down The Road Less Traveled. You are the vehicle. If the rain starts coming down outside, if you start having hard times in your life, if you feel as though the world is raining on your parade, you can turn on your windshield wipers and seek help. Read or associate yourself with positive friends or helpful family members, teachers, and mentors. Get all the help you need to help you at the task of attaining your goal. The role of the windshield wiper is to support you through the times when you can't see clearly and to assist you in focusing on your goals. The windshield wiper is to help you help yourself. So, when the rain turns into a little drizzle and you feel like you can handle it on your own you can turn it off. You are the vehicle to your destiny.

You are a special vehicle because you are one of a kind. Your vehicle is chameleon like. It becomes the kind of vehicle that you need at the time, if you need to speed things up in life your vehicle becomes a sports car, if you are going through some rocky times your vehicle becomes a multipurpose vehicle to help you through the mountains of life. If you have a lot on your mind your vehicle becomes a truck so it can carry the load of discomfort to a field of solidarity. You are the vehicle to your destiny. So, as you travel the road to your endeavors look long and hard at who you want to be and the opportunities that you want to make for yourself. Prior to switching lanes, reach in your glove compartment and pull out your mental map. Where do you want to go, who do you want to be? You are the vehicle to your destiny. You have the power. Empower yourself to be all that you can be.

Empowerment

CHAPTER 10

Throughout your life you may encounter obstacles while traveling the road to your destiny. Obstacles that will lead you to the treasures of life as well as obstacles promoting emotional heartache. As a child you encountered many different obstacles and developed many different skills and points of view. The excitement that you put forth in life has lent it's hand in guiding you to the place where you now stand. The aspirations that you have developed for yourself are a direct result of your position in life. During each stage of your life there has been some sort of transformation. Change is growth and growth is change. You only change and grow if you have the desire. That is, if you are incessant about making a change. You are the vehicle to your destiny. However, your vehicle will go no where without gas. Your vehicle will stay in neutral if you do not maneuver your hand to pull down the gear shift into drive. You are the one in power. In fact, you empower yourself and your vehicle, hence you have the power to reach your destiny. In accordance with the destiny of being good, one big step that you have to take is to take charge of your life. This is a very difficult concept for many people because they forget that taking charge of your life requires taking responsibility. Empowering yourself and responsibility go hand and hand like cold in ice. They are a couple

•

that will never divorce. Taking charge of your life is saying that you are going to go after what makes you happy, going after who you want to be. You want to do things that are going to make you a better person as well as promote the people around you. Empowering yourself is making the statement and commitment that you are the only one who is going to make it happen. Taking responsibility is saying, "Whatever happens is a direct result of the effort that I put into it."

There are many people who go through life blaming other people for the situation that they are in. There are people who are evicted from their homes and blame the landlord. Players are cut from the basketball team and blame the coach. There are people who fail an academic course and blame the teacher. There are people that will fall down and blame the sidewalk.

You can blame the world for the negative situations that you are in, or you can empower yourself. Take the responsibility for what happens, so if you get an A in a course then you are responsible. You are responsible for studying at night. You are responsible for asking your teacher or mentor for help and support. You are responsible for putting in the extra effort that earned an A. Empowering yourself allows you to take full responsibility for you good and bad. Once you start taking full responsibility for yourself you can see that in any situation, you have the power to make it different. When I say different I mean that you have the power to make it better. Better does not mean easy, it means different. Better does not mean that everything is going to come out roses. Better means that you are closer to becoming a good person. Closer to becoming the person you want to be. Closer to becoming good.

Empower yourself and take charge of your life. Do not succumb to the defeatist attitudes that are placed upon you. Make attempts to walk away from the role of victim in life situations. Yes, life can knock you down, beat you up, kick you all around, but remember that when life does knock you down, you have the choice of getting back up.

•

When life deals you a bad hand you can cry or you can try. When life throws in the towel on your emotional boxing match you have the choice to continue training for the next opportunity for success. When life turns it's back on you, you can follow the role of Simba and his friends from Lion King, the animated movie, and say, "Hakuna Matata" (nothing matters) and turn your back on life. You can stare life dead in the face and say out loud, "I will not quit. I will not stop. I am somebody. I will be somebody. I am responsible for me and the road to my destiny." You are responsible for your destiny. You are the king of your world. You have the power and you are empowered.

Empowered, means you have the energy, all the energy that you need to get you where you want to go. Be careful how you use your energy. Many people choose to use their energy to focus on the negativities of life, focusing on who has stopped them from succeeding. Many people burn up energy by holding grudges. These things use up energy and take you in a direction that is not helping you reach the goal of being a productive member of society. If you use these same energies in a positive flow you can ride the positive bandwagon into a direction that will allow you to bring people up instead of putting them down. You can release the negative energy of holding grudges and staying mad and can focus on the positive, on the things that matter.

Do not spend lots of energy worrying about something you cannot change. You will find it much more advantageous to spend that time and energy concentrating on the things that you can change. Some people focus on what they want to stop doing, or stop seeing, and everything they don't want to do. This is a waste of energy. Spend your time and energy focusing on what you want to do. When you focus on the yes, it is positive, when you focus on the no, it is negative. Ride the wave of yes. Say, "Yes, I can. Yes, I will be successful as an engineer. Yes, I will go to college. Yes, I will go to class. Yes, I will treat my body in a manner which will promote good health.

"Refrain from catering to the cancerous, stagnating disability called limitation."

———————— • ————————

I WANT TO
BE GOOD

I will care for myself and respect myself. Yes I will empower myself because I am responsible for me and I am a responsible person. I am all that I can be." The reality is that you have the power. You have the power to be anything you want to be, the power to go anywhere you want to go. You have the power to change your present situation no matter what it is. If you are relying on someone else to give you your dream, to make the change for you; you are in fact relying on a tow truck that may never come. You are the vehicle to your destiny. Empower yourself to be all that you can be. You have the power to be good.

TOOLS TO USE

1) Use I statements when talking, such as, "I will take charge of my life."

2) In every situation that has disappointed you, look for something positive and use that to build yourself up.

Just Good

CHAPTER 11

Super, fantastic, awesome, are all moments in your life. Good is a lifetime. You have a fantastic school year. You have an awesome athletic season. Good is a lifetime. Good is day-in and day-out. Good is looking at and evaluating yourself. When you are able to say that at least 51% of the time I was good then you have achieved good. I am a good man. Use the tools that are going to make you good.

Take the direction in life so that you are able to look in the mirror and say, "Today is a great day and I am good." Drive your vehicle to your destiny. Remember that each day you are on this planet is a day unto itself. Yesterday is in the past, it cannot be recaptured, you cannot physically step into yesterday. Tomorrow has not yet happened. You cannot capture tomorrow. You cannot step into tomorrow physically. You cannot change tomorrow, and you cannot change yesterday. Focus on what and how you can make a difference now. So, as you go through life being the person that you want to be, live each day as a special day. Treat each day as the only day that you have, for today is your future's history. You cannot change the past but you can change your future's history, which is actually the present. Live each day in the present. Take advantage of today. Today is a great day, a new day. The only day like it on this earth. It is an opportunity to grow, to live, an opportunity to be good. You can work on your goals today. Today is what matters. Today is what determines where you will be tomorrow, if tomorrow is granted to you. Today is what matters. Take the steps to be all you can be. To be GOOD. Like L.P. McKellar says, "If you are good each moment, then in the end you will be awesome, super, and fantastic."

"A dream is merely a goal with an expiration date."

———————— • ————————

I WANT TO
BE GOOD

End Note

FOR SABRINA

A note to my daughter, Sabrina. When I started this book you had not yet met with conception. As I come to completion of this book you are actively moving about in your Mommy's tummy. A place where your three brothers got their start. Mine and your Mommy's thoughts of you, as you are swimming about in the womb, are thoughts of excitement. You are our first daughter and your brother's first sister. You are going to have three older brothers which will present some challenges in itself, but will also provide protection. Five year old Jonathan talks about you all the time. Three year old Kevin has ordered you out of Mommy's tummy three times by saying, "Sabrina, you come out right now." Two year old Stephen says. "I want a little sister as long as I can have my own room." We are all waiting for you, Sabrina, and I wanted to drop you a line in this book. My wish is that all goes well as you travel into this world. I look forward to the time that we will share on this planet together. Sabrina, maybe my next book will be about you. As I think of you, and your mother, and both your grandmothers, I think of the word good. When I look in the eyes of your mother and reminisce about growing up with your grandmother McKellar, and as I interact with your grandmother Lake, I think of good being short. Short not because these women are physically short. Short because these three women, had a hand in bringing you into this world. Good is like a blanket that leaves your feet exposed on the cold days of winter, it is too short. Too short of a word to hold next to the likes of women like your mother and your grandmothers. I don't know what the word is, maybe it is good plus, plus, but you are a part of them. Sabrina, I am looking forward to you, your brothers are looking for-ward to you, your mother is looking forward to you and I hope that you enjoy this little place called earth.

I love you,
Daddy.

About The Author

———————————————— ● ————————————————

Mr. McKellar is a therapist by training and speaker by desire. He has produced the popular audio tapes YOU ARE THE VEHICLE TO YOUR DESTINY and WHERE YOUR MIND GOES YOU BODY WILL FOLLOW. He can be found making presentations across the country. His dynamic speaking style has captured the attention of the young and old alike. He has performed in front of audiences as large as 5000. His humor and wit leave you spellbound. Realizing that the sky is no longer the limit, Mr. McKellar motivates everyone to reach for the stars. Mr. McKellar received his under graduate degree from West Virginia University, where he studied psychology and was a member of the WVU football team. Mr. McKellar went on to receive his Masters degree from Hood College. He has extensive therapeutic experience working with children and their families. Ken is a practitioner of hypno therapy and is certified in Neuro Linguistic Programming (NLP) and is looking forward to starting work on his Ph.D. He is an active member of Toastmasters where he continues to grow and help the growth of others as a communicator. Mr. McKellar's ultimate goal is to help cultivate positive change in the lives of young people.

———————————————— ● ————————————————